Linus Pierpont Brockett

The Philanthropic Results of the War in America

Collected from official and other authentic sources

Linus Pierpont Brockett

The Philanthropic Results of the War in America
Collected from official and other authentic sources

ISBN/EAN: 9783337011734

Printed in Europe, USA, Canada, Australia, Japan

Cover: Foto ©ninafisch / pixelio.de

More available books at **www.hansebooks.com**

THE

PHILANTHROPIC RESULTS

OF

THE WAR IN AMERICA,

COLLECTED FROM OFFICIAL AND OTHER AUTHENTIC SOURCES,

BY

AN AMERICAN CITIZEN.

NEW YORK:

PRESS OF WYNKOOP, HALLENBECK & THOMAS,

No. 113 FULTON STREET.

1863.

WAR IN AMERICA.

The Proclamation of the President of the United States, on the 15th of April, 1861, announcing the fall of Fort Sumter, and calling for troops to defend the nation from treason and rebellion, found an instant response in the nation's heart. Not only did the brave and stalwart men of the Republic offer themselves in numbers far beyond the Government's demand, but treasure was poured out like water, for the supply of all the wants of the army which was to be created for the suppression of the rebellion.

The Legislatures of most of the loyal States met in extra session, and without waiting to see whether there was any probability that the national treasury would reimburse their expenditure,* voted large sums for arming and equipping troops. The aggregate amounts

---

* The credit of the national treasury was, at this time, sadly impaired by the gross mismanagement of the Secretary of the Treasury under the former administration (Howell Cobb), who had finally filled up the measure of his crimes by adding treason to his malfeasance in office.

thus advanced by the States, within three weeks after the President's proclamation, was $23,240,000. This was no unwilling contribution wrung by the hand of arbitrary power from the hard earnings of the people; on the contrary, it was offered without urgency, except by the people themselves; the sums fixed upon were voted with hardly a dissenting voice, and the action of the several Legislatures met with the most hearty approval from their constituents.

About $12,000,000 of the amount was subsequently refunded by the General Government. The border States, Delaware, Maryland, Kentucky and Missouri, and the Pacific States, California and Oregon, did not at this time, make any legislative grants.

But the liberality displayed in furnishing money for the equipment of soldiers at this first outbreak of the war, was not confined to the Legislatures; nearly every city and considerable town throughout the loyal States made its subscription, both by vote of its municipal authorities, and by the spontaneous contributions of its business corporations and its citizens. Before the 6th of May, 1861, New York city had contributed $2,173,000; Philadelphia, $330,000; Boston, $168,000; Cincinnati, $280,000; Buffalo, $110,000, and other cities and towns in like proportion. An imperfect list, which gave less than half the cities and towns which had subscribed for the equipment of troops, showed an aggregate of $4,877,000. The entire amount must have considerably exceeded $7,000,000. From these two sources, then, in the first three weeks of the rebellion, was an aggregate contribution of over $30,000,000, to the fitting out of the volunteer army. After deducting the $12,000,000 refunded by the United States Government, there still remained more than $18,000,000 of absolute donation.

It may be said that this was no deliberate, well-considered liberality, springing from generous principle, but the result of a wild, frantic excitement, from which the sober second thought of the nation revolted, and which was the subject of subsequent regrets. The history of the time proves just the reverse.

It was soon found that the task of quelling the rebellion was one of gigantic proportions; that the conspirators had been for years maturing their plans, and that their treason could only be crushed out by the array of an overwhelming force. In his message of July 4, President Lincoln suggested the propriety of calling for 400,000 men, and voting $400,000,000 for the work. Congress responded by authorizing calls for one million of men,* and $500,000,000. The work of raising and equipping such an army was entirely beyond the experience of any man in this country; beyond, indeed, the experience of any men of modern times; for large as

---

* Congress probably intended to authorize the raising of only 500,000; but, in reality, two separate acts, July 22 and July 25, were passed, each authorizing the raising of 500,000 men. Under these acts, 780,000 were actually raised.

some of the armies of modern Europe have been, no single power had called a million of new troops into the field within a twelvemonth.

While the Government disbursed liberally for the bounties, uniforms, equipment, arming, and rations for these troops, there were other expenses connected with the organizations of the regiments which were met from private or municipal sources, of very large amount in the aggregate, larger in some regiments than others; but in those from Eastern States averaging somewhat more than $25,000 (some regiments cost over $75,000), and in the Western States from $15,000 to $20,000. The regiments thus raised to January, 1862, were a little more than eight hundred, and the aggregate recruiting by individuals and corporations was over $16,000,000.

Attention was early called to the sanitary condition and wants of the army, and already, in the early part of the summer of 1861, large sums of money and supplies of all sorts—havelocks to protect them from sunstroke, woollen socks, and undershirts, rubber blankets, and clothing for hospital purposes, dried fruits, books, pamphlets, and newspapers)—were contributed for the improvement of the health and morals of the soldiers. There were already hospitals for sick soldiers, and to these large contributions were made of such articles as the medical department, under its existing regulations, could not furnish. But it was not till after the battle of Bull Run, July 21, 1861, that the necessity for enlarged liberality in providing for the sick and wounded soldier began to be felt, and the promptness with which supplies were forwarded to the hospitals of Washington and Alexandria on that occasion, and the readiness with which the most skillful physicians and surgeons, and the most competent nurses, volunteered their services, without fee or reward, demonstrated most conclusively that it was no evanescent impulse, but a fixed principle of patriotism, which moved the national heart.

The sympathy of the people with the nation's defenders was manifested also in another direction. When, on the 20th of April, the New York Seventh Militia, the Massachusetts Eighth, and several other regiments, on their way to the defense of Washington, reached Philadelphia, and there learned of the brutal attack of the mob upon the Massachusetts Sixth Regiment, at Baltimore, they were detained for twelve hours in Philadelphia, and patriotic citizens of that city, many of them of the humbler classes, ministered freely to their wants. As other regiments passed through the city, a noble-hearted man, Mr. B. S. Brown, undertook to provide hot coffee for them, and his neighbors contributed cold ham, bread, butter, and other articles of food, and as regiments came almost every night, it grew into a custom, that upon the firing of a signal-gun, announcing the approach of a regiment, the people in the vicinity of the Navy Yard, where the regiments

landed, assembled, many of them after wearisome
toil through the day, and welcomed the soldiers,
and provided liberally for their comfort and wants.
The citizens of Philadelphia contributed freely for the
maintenance of this spontaneous charity, and there are
to-day two vast structures, each capable of feeding a
half regiment at once, known as the Union Volunteer
Refreshment Saloon, and the Cooper Shop Refreshment Saloon, to which the wearied soldier, going to the
field or returning from the scene of his triumphs, is
welcomed, and provided with abundance of water for
washing away the dust and stains of travel, an ample
repast, made more grateful by the fair hands which
minister to his wants, and, if sick or wounded, a
comfortable bed, and attendance—for hospitals have
grown up in connection with these saloons—where the
sick or wounded soldier may find the best of care.* It
was characteristic of the feeling of sympathy which
actuated the masses that, in Philadelphia, the firemen
said to each other, when the wounded were brought to
their city, and carried in hired conveyances to the hospitals : " These poor fellows deserve tenderer care and
handling than they will receive from hired hackmen ;
we will build ambulances for them, and carry them to
the hospitals ourselves." To this thoughtfulness it is
owing that there are now twenty-six of these ambulances, luxurious affairs, costing from $500 to $800 each,

---

* See Appendix II.

drawn by two horses, and kept always ready in the engine houses of the fire companies for the transportation of sick and wounded, and that in these they are carried, attended by firemen, and handled as gently as a mother would handle her infant, to the hospitals, and without any compensation. The various plans for the relief of the sick and wounded soldiers took form and shape in a variety of organizations during the summer and autumn of 1861, each crystallizing around some central idea or purpose of local or general character, but all having in view the soldier's welfare.

(The United States Sanitary Commission, created June 9, 1861, by an order of the Secretary of War,) in consequence of the solicitation of Rev. Dr. Bellows, Dr. R. C. Wood, acting Surgeon-General of the Army, and others, not only ministered to the comfort and watched over the health of the soldier in the camp, but distributed its counsels in regard to the location and preparation of camps, the preparation of food, the maintenance of cleanliness, protection from miasma, and the treatment of surgical and medical diseases of the camps, and at the same time gathered and distributed supplies of lint, bandages, medicines, cordials, delicacies, and hospital clothing and furniture for those in the hospitals. * The Western Sanitary Commission, created by an order of Major-General Fremont, September 5, 1861, performed a similar work at the

---

* See Appendix *A.*

West; * the (Christian Alliance furnished religious and moral reading, newspapers, books, and magazines to the sick and well;) the Bible and Tract Societies distributed copies of the New Testament, hymn books, religious books, and tracts among them, † and all over the land, Soldiers' Relief, Soldiers' Aid, and Union Relief Societies collected stores of clothing and delicacies for the sick, and employed the hearts, hands, and heads of tens of thousands of patriotic women in labors of love, for the benefit of the soldiers in the field and in the hospital.‡

There was another direction in which there was a call for large-handed liberality. While the pay of the volunteer soldiers was liberal, and decidedly higher than that of other nations, and was in many cases a higher compensation than had been received by some of the volunteers in civil life, it was with many others much less than their previous earnings, and from the financial difficulties of the Government at the beginning of the war, was not, for many months, so promptly paid as it should have been; and the greedy sutler and the gambler were ready to fleece the soldier of his pay in advance, and without any just equivalent. Hence it happened, that in many cases the families of the soldiers were in danger of suffering for want of the means of support, and in some cases did suffer. To alleviate this distress was felt to be a duty, and in some States, the State authori-

---

* See appendix *B*.   † See appendix *D*.   ‡ See appendices *F* and *G*.

ties, in others, the counties or towns, and in all, individuals, gave liberally to the support of the families of volunteers. Usually this assistance was in the form of a weekly, or monthly stipend to the wife, sisters, or mother of the soldier, which was increased if there were children dependent on them for support. In many cases, also, food, clothing, medicines, and medical attendance were contributed. The aggregate of these appropriations was very large : in the city of New York, up to May, 1863, $2,500,000 had been appropriated by the city government, beside about $250,000 from the Union Defense Fund; in Brooklyn, N. Y., $1,000,000; in Philadelphia, $1,500,000; in Baltimore, nearly $400,000; while the cities and towns of Massachusetts have given $4,315,285 for the purpose; Illinois, over a million; Maine, $2,750,000; Connecticut, from the State treasury alone, $834,076; Vermont, in extra pay to the soldiers for their families $1,125,000, and other States in proportion. The amount from all the States, including payments of counties, cities, towns, and individuals, has exceeded $25,000,000.

During the year 1862 there were many severe battles, in different portions of the extended region occupied by the armed forces, some of them attended by great loss of life and numerous casualties. At the West, the battles of Mill Spring, Fort Donelson, Shiloh, the capture of Island No. Ten, Corinth, Memphis, and New Orleans, the battles of Fayetteville, Baton Rouge,

Cane Hill, Arkansas Post, Munfordsville, Chaplin Hills, Iuka, and Stone River; and in the East, Williamsburgh, West Point, Fair Oaks, Winchester, Cross Keys, Port Republic, the Seven Days, Cedar Mountain, Centreville, Groveton, Chantilly, South Mountain, Antietam, and Fredericksburgh, as well as many skirmishes and actions of less note, kept the hospitals filled with the wounded, and the pestilential swamps of the Chickahominy proved more fatal to both the Federal and Confederate army than the battle-field. While the medical department of the army did what it could to alleviate the vast suffering so heroically endured by our brave soldiers, its newly developed resources were constantly overtasked, and there was a wide field for humane effort in supplying to the hospitals the necessary furniture and stores, and to the men suitable changes, clothing in place of that soiled and torn on the battle-field, new dressings, and those delicacies, drinks, and aliments absolutely necessary for the successful treatment of the sick.

Here, again, there was occasion for an appeal to the liberality of the people, and like all those which had preceded it, it was answered by a lavish outpouring of money, supplies, and personal service, which showed most conclusively that it was a pleasure to give. In some of the States, a contingent fund was placed in the hands of the Governor, to be expended for the care and removal of the sick and wounded; in others, special appropriations of large amount were made for the purpose; in all, the spontaneous contributions, in the churches, at public gatherings, and in response to appeals through the public prints, were so abundant that there was no lack wherever the supplies could be forwarded. The Pacific States, which, from their remote position, had not hitherto been called upon for assistance, responded to the appeal of the Sanitary Commission by a contribution of over half a million dollars; and from every quarter the supplies poured into the treasuries of the organizations for their distribution, in the greatest abundance. In most of the large cities, and in many of the smaller ones, hospitals for soldiers were established; and while the Government supplied the rations and medicines, the people supplied everything else. Washington had twenty-three of these hospitals, Philadelphia, thirty-two; New York and Brooklyn, fifteen; Boston, five; and Cincinnati, Louisville, Chicago, St. Louis, Indianapolis, Davenport, Keokuk, and other Western cities, each a considerable number.

But more beautiful and touching than these munificent gifts of money or supplies, were the offers of personal service. Physicians and surgeons, the most eminent in their profession, men whose services commanded hundreds of dollars per day, volunteered by scores to go to the battle-field or the temporary hospital, and exerted their best skill for the care and healing of the coun-

try's defenders. Immediately after the battle of Antietam, forty of the most eminent physicians of New York
city started for the battle-field. Clergymen, pastors of
large and wealthy congregations, sought the opportu-
nity of ministering to the sick and dying soldier, of
breathing into the ear, fast growing dull to earthly
sounds, the words of spiritual consolation, and of receiving from lips soon to become silent in death, utter-
ances of faith and messages of love. Senators and Representatives in Congress; Judges of the highest Courts,
and members of the bar, of the most brilliant reputa-
tion, sought, in ministrations to these wounded and dying heroes, to taste the luxury of doing good. Among
those not connected with the learned professions, too,
there was the same earnestness and self-sacrifice. Men
and women occupying the highest social position, and
of large wealth, devoted themselves for many consecu-
tive months to the nursing of the sick, watching over
them, ministering to them as tenderly as if members of
their own households; and in many instances, fair
maidens and comely matrons, who a year or two before
were leaders in fashion and gayety, kneeled with blood-
soiled garments, to wipe the death-damps from the
brow of the dying volunteer; and those who before,
would have shuddered at the sight of death, even in its
most placid form, became familiar with its horrors in
the crowded hospital, or on the field of carnage. On
that gory field of Antietam, on the right wing, where

the dead of Hooker's, and Mansfield's, and Sumner's, and Franklin's corps lay thickest, from the early dawn till midnight, a young and gentle woman, in whose veins flowed some of the best blood of Massachusetts, toiled as few men could have done, staunching wounds which might otherwise have proved fatal, administering cordials to the fainting soldier, cheering those destined to undergo amputation, moistening lips parching with thirst, giving nourishing food to those who had sunk from wounds and exhaustion, and ever and anon, closing eyes that had looked their last upon earth, or receiving and noting messages of love to absent ones, from those about to depart to the silent land. Nor was this her first experience of the battle-field. On that succession of battles before Washington in August, so constant and valuable had been her ministrations, that the surgeons named her the " angel of the battle-field." Many as are the uses of money, and much as it could do for the suffering soldier, how worthless do gifts of it seem beside such sacrifices as these !*

Among the other enterprises undertaken for the benefit of wounded soldiers, was one which deserved success, and whose failure was a matter of reproach to the military commander and the civilians by whom that failure was occasioned; it was a project for an ambulance and hospital corps, to be composed of men enlisted for the purpose, and attached, to the number

---

* See Appendix I.

of about twenty, to each regiment, capable, in case of emergency, of doing their part in fighting, but having in charge the ambulances, litters, and stretchers, belonging to the corps, and specially trained to bring wounded men off the field, to administer to them cordials when needed, to check hemorrhage by the application of a temporary tourniquet; to preserve the valuables and mementoes of the slain, for after-identification, and in camp to act as nurses, hospital stewards, and attendants.

The projector of the system was an eminent teacher of New York,* who, like many others, had devoted months to the care of the sick and wounded, and from the results of his experience had matured his plan with great care, and with the advice and approval of the most eminent military and civil officers of the Government; it was thoroughly practical, and would unquestionably have saved hundreds, if not thousands, of precious lives, but the aversion of the Commander-in-Chief to any measures or plans which departed from the ordinary routine of military practice led him to oppose his powerful influence to it, and caused its defeat in the Senate. Its projector had labored unwearingly, and at great personal sacrifice, for months, for its success, but its failure led to no relaxation of his efforts in behalf of the soldier.

Among other forms in which the earnest sympathy

---

* Appendix J.

of the people with the army found utterance, was the organization of the Christian Commission. The Young Men's Christian Associations of the principal cities of the North had, from the commencement of the war, contributed largely, both of men and means, to the country's service, and had been especially active in collecting and forwarding supplies for the sick and wounded on the battle-field.

In November, 1861, at a convention of these associations, the organization of an Executive Commission which should unite and extend the work which had previously been done by the associations separately, was resolved upon; it did not, however, come into active operation till the spring of 1862. Its principal objects are the care of the physical health and welfare of the soldier, the care of the sick and wounded, the moral culture and improvement and religious instruction of both classes, and their protection from frauds and wrongs. Its agents are all voluntary and unpaid, except the mere cost of living, and the large amount of supplies distributed by it are forwarded without cost to the givers or to the recipients. During the year and five months (to June 1) of its existence, it has employed about six hundred delegates, lay and clerical, and has expended over $100,000 in money, and distributed nearly $400,000 in supplies, receiving voluntary services from railroad companies, telegraph lines, and individuals, valued at not less than $100,000 more. No

3

appeal which it has made to the public for contributions has ever failed to meet with a hearty response.*

Another class of organizations which accomplished
no small amount of good among the soldiers, were the
Missionary Societies.† The American Missionary
Association; the Free Mission Society; the American
Baptist Home Mission Society; the two American
Tract Societies (of Boston and New York); the
American Sunday School Union, and, perhaps, some
other religious societies have had their missionaries
and colporteurs among the soldiers, who have rendered
valuable services to their physical and moral welfare.
The American Bible Society; the Episcopal Book and
Tract Society; the Presbyterian Board of Publication;
the Presbyterian (N. S.) Publication Committee; the
Reformed Dutch Board of Publication, as well as the
several Tract Societies, &c., have also made large grants
of religious books for distribution in the army. ‡

The local organizations which have contributed
money and supplies, independently of the Sanitary or
Christian Commissions, are so numerous that we can
only mention the largest. At St. Louis, the Western
Sanitary Commission has disbursed in money $155,000,
and in supplies $395,000, or together $550,000.§ In
most of the States of the West there are Sanitary
organizations not connected with the United States
Sanitary Commission. That of Illinois, having its

---

* See Appendix C. † See Appendix E. ‡ See Appendix D.
§ See Appendix B.

headquarters at Chicago, has expended $42,714 in money, and a little over $300,000 in supplies; that of Indiana, over $100,000; that of Iowa about $58,000.

Soldiers' Homes or Rests, places where the soldier, going to the army, or returning on furlough, sick, or dis· charged, can find comfortable quarters, good meals, and friends who will procure for him his bounty, back pay or pensions, and who will secure for him transporta· tion, &c., all without compensation, and thus protect him from the sharpers who lie in wait in all the large cities to plunder the unsuspecting soldier, have been established in all the principal cities East and West. We have reports of four in New York, three in Phila· delphia, one in Baltimore, two in Washington, and one or more in Pittsburgh, Wheeling, Cleveland, Colum· bus, Cincinnati, Chicago, Indianapolis, St. Louis, Louis· ville, Cairo, Memphis,* &c., &c.

Of other organizations, the New England Soldiers' Relief Association, founded by sons of New England resident in New York, April 3, 1862, is one of the largest. Its disbursements in the past fourteen months, have been very large both in money and supplies. There are also agencies, partly defrayed by the States and partly by individual contributions, for the care of the soldiers of most of the loyal States. The Ladies' Aid Society of Philadelphia, one of the earliest and most efficient of its class, has expended about $44,000 in

---

* Appendix II.

money, and not far from $200,000 in supplies. There are several other similar, but smaller organizations in Philadelphia and its vicinity. The Union Relief Association of Baltimore has disbursed in money and supplies not far from $50,000.* In Washington there are sixteen so-called State Relief Associations, composed of citizens of Washington or temporary residents there, formerly from the different States. These associations have contributed liberally themselves, and have received supplies and money from the States which they represent, which they have distributed by their own committees, without cost, to the soldiers of their respective States, in the hospitals and on the field. The amounts thus distributed are estimated by these associations at a little more than $1,000,000. Aside from these, there have been distributed by ladies resident in Washington, supplies received from friends and local associations at the North, not otherwise credited, to the amount, as ascertained by the most careful and moderate estimates, of $1,045,000. At St. Louis, Louisville, Cairo, Nashville, and on the battle-fields of the West, similar distributions have been made in very large amounts; in hundreds of instances, towns and cities raising money and supplies in amounts varying from $500 to $5,000, and sending them to the field after a battle, by a voluntary, unpaid agent from among their own citizens. After the battle of Shiloh alone, it is estimated by cautious

---

* Appendices F. and G.

men, thoroughly conversant with the facts, that supplies to the amount of over half a million of dollars were
forwarded from the Northwestern States. Even
while we write, intelligence comes that in Illinois, in
answer to an appeal issued May 27, 1863, by the State
Commissioner-General, for wounded soldiers, there were
received in nine days $12,500 in money, contributed by
small towns, only one of them having so many as
five thousand inhabitants, and more than five times
that amount in supplies. This, be it remembered, was
after not less than a dozen previous calls, for the same
purpose, each of which had been as liberally answered.
The aggregate amount of this class of contributions
cannot be estimated with any approach to accuracy ;
and the chief danger in any estimate which may be
made, is of putting the amount much below the truth.
A General of the army stationed for some time at Cairo,
and subsequently attached in turn, to the army of the
Mississippi, the army of the Ohio, and the army of the
Cumberland, gave it as his opinion, the result of extensive and careful observation, that these contributions
exceeded $5,000,000, and others whose opportunities
for observation were as good, concurred in the estimate.

The disasters which befel the army of the Potomac,
and the extraordinary exertions made by the Confederate authorities to call into the field as large a force as
possible, led the President, in July, 1862, to issue a call
for three hundred thousand three-years' troops, and in

August, a second, for three hundred thousand more, for nine months. An enrollment was ordered, preparatory to a draft, which it was supposed would be necessary for raising the second quota, but great exertions were made by the States, counties, and individuals to encourage volunteering, by the offer of liberal bounties, extra pay, and provision for families, and in most of the States, these exertions were so far successful, that the quotas were nearly or quite filled without resort to conscription. The sums raised for bounties, &c., were in many of the States very large; in New York, the State offered a bounty of $50; the county of New York $50 additional, the county of Kings $60, and some of the other counties $75 or $100, while the subscriptions of wards, districts, and individuals, increased the amount in some instances to $250 or even $300. The average bounty paid in the State was computed to be over $150 per man, aside from that offered by the General Government. In several of the New England States this amount was exceeded. In Rhode Island, and in Massachusetts, and Connecticut, in many towns, the amount of bounty (with the State appropriation) was $300, $330, and in one or two cases as high as $375 per man, and the average for these three States was over $200. In Philadelphia an appropriation of $500,000 was made by the city, and a fund raised, by subscription, of $486,270.49 for the purpose of paying bounties, and aiding the families of the volunteers. In most of the

Western States the amount paid for bounties was very large. In many instances pledges were given by wealthy citizens to pay specified sums monthly to the families of volunteers. An approximate estimate of the amount of these bounties, gives an aggregate of $34,300,000.

The claims of another class, reduced to destitution by the war, to be relieved, were beginning to press upon the consideration of the charitable. In those sections of the Southern States, invaded and occupied by our troops, the slaveholders, when compelled, from their active participation in the rebellion, to abandon their estates, left, for the most part, the feeble and infirm slaves upon their plantations—the old or sickly women, and the young children—and compelled the able-bodied slaves, the "prime hands," as they were called, to go with them to the interior, or sold them in the States where slavery was yet regarded as safe. Many of these afterward escaped, and came into the employ of the Union forces in various capacities. But the feeble and infirm could not be suffered to perish; and arrangements were made, under Government direction, to employ such of them as were able to work, on the plantations which had been abandoned, or in work in the vicinity of the camps, and to allow moderate rations for their sustenance. It was found, however, very soon, that they needed clothing, superintendence, schools for the children, &c., &c.; and while, so far as they were able, they were willing to pay moderate prices for these supplies, a considerable portion must be donated. Freedmen's Relief Societies were accordingly organized in Boston, New York, Philadelphia, Cincinnati, Chicago and St. Louis; and clothing, agricultural implements, books of instruction, &c., &c., forwarded to them. The Bible and religious publication societies also sent them many simple reading books, Testaments, &c.; and the missionary societies sent missionaries and teachers to instruct them. The aggregate expenditures for all these purposes, including clothing furnished, &c., is about $540,000.

There was still another appeal to the sympathies of the nation, and this time from over the sea. The sudden falling off of imports from England and France, at the commencement of the war, leaving many of the manufacturers for a time, without a market for their goods, occasioned much embarrassment and many failures among them; and before the surplus of goods had been exhausted, the rapid rise in the price of cotton, resulting from the necessary state of blockade, rendered production unprofitable, and the subsequent scarcity of that staple made it impossible to keep the mills employed. Under these circumstances nearly four hundred thousand of the operatives in the cotton mills of Lancashire and Derbyshire, and those dependent upon them, were thrown out of employment, and soon began to suffer from starvation. They bore up bravely under their privations as long as it was possible; and fully

satisfied that the war in this country to put down a rebellion caused by, and based upon slavery, was a just
one, they steadily refused to throw the blame of their
sufferings upon the United States Government, though
often solicited to do so by English sympathizers with
the South. Their condition was daily growing more
desperate; and though subscriptions for their relief
were made in England to the amount of $9,000,000 or
$10,000,000, there was still a large amount of suffering
to be relieved. The loyal American people felt that it
was due to themselves that they should manifest their
hearty sympathy with their brethren in distress, especially since that distress had grown, in part at least, out
of the inevitable consequences of the war, and those
who were the chief sufferers from it had been their
firm friends under the most trying circumstances. The
movement for sending aid to them was hailed with joy
in all quarters; contributions poured in from all the
principal cities, and from country towns as well.

An eminent shipping house offered a new and capa-
cious vessel, to bear the gifts of the nation to England;
it was soon freighted and dispatched, but could not
carry all that was offered. The Corn Exchange freighted (in part) another vessel, and a considerable amount
was forwarded in bills of exchange. Philadelphia also
contributed a ship-load of provisions to these sufferers.
The aggregate amount contributed for the relief of the
Lancashire and Derbyshire operatives, was about

4

$265,000. A few thousand dollars were also contribu-
ted for the French operatives of the Department of
Seine Inferieure, Rouen, &c., who were suffering, though
in a less degree.

But the charities of the nation did not stop here.
No sooner were supplies forwarded to the English
operatives, than it was found that extensive suffering
and incipient starvation were threatening a large portion of the manufacturing districts in Ireland, and that
but little aid was bestowed upon them by the English
Government or people. The Irish people were bound
to us by strong ties; they had offered their services
without stint, for the war, and on every battle-field
they had proved their valor, and shed their blood. We
could not turn a deaf ear to their appeals for help, and
again, and up to the present time, contributions have
flowed in freely for their assistance, and more than
$100,000 have been raised for their relief.

Amid all these demands upon the liberality of a
noble and generous people, it is a fact of deep interest,
that no one of the charitable organizations of a peace-
ful time has been stinted; the orphan asylums, homes
for the friendless, asylums for the aged and indigent,
the dispensaries, infirmaries, and hospitals, the associations for the relief of the poor, and all those charities
which have their claims upon the public, alike in times
of peace and war, have been abundantly supported, and
many new ones for the relief and maintenance of the

children of deceased or disabled soldiers, or for giving to the crippled soldier himself a home, where he may spend the evening of life in quiet and comfort, have sprung up and received large contributions. The great religious societies, whether national or denominational, have had a larger income than in times of peace, schools and colleges have been amply supported, and many of the latter liberally endowed ; the salaries of the clergy have been very generally increased, and in hundreds of instances debts, which had crippled the activity and impaired the usefulness of churches and congregations have been paid off during the past year.

Our volunteer soldiers have not been unmindful of the responsibilities which the nation's trust and large-hearted liberality has imposed on them. An Act of Congress has been passed providing that the soldier may, under certain regulations which render fraud impossible, allot such portion of his pay as he desires, for the benefit of his family, or those dependent upon him, and in several of the States, citizens of the highest character and standing have given their services without fee or reward as commissioners, to visit the regiments, and procure from the men allotments for their families. In the State of New York, as a result of this effort, over $6,000,000 per annum is thus forwarded to soldiers' families ; in several of the other States, the amount though smaller, is in about the same proportion to troops they have in the field. In the aggregate, more than $16,000,000 per annum is thus saved from the greed of the sutler, or the rapacity of the gamblers, and other harpies, who always follow an army to plunder its soldiers.

In this hasty sketch of the charities evoked by the war, we have necessarily omitted all mention of many of the active organizations which have devoted themselves to the welfare of the soldiers; and have, of course, been unable to give even an approximate statement of the vast amount contributed directly by individuals to the objects of their beneficence.* We have, however, as we believe, demonstrated conclusively, that, neither in ancient or modern times, has there been so vast an outpouring of a nation's wealth for the care, the comfort, and the physical and moral welfare of those who have fought the nation's battles or been the sufferers from its condition of war.

While then, in this regard, the record of the United States is one which confers the highest honor upon its humanity, its philanthropy, and its patriotism, it is yet, when viewed aright, no matter of surprise that the national heart should have been thus stirred to its innermost depths; for never, in the history of the human

---

* One form of contribution, very large in amount, but from the nature of the case not capable of being estimated statistically, is deserving of notice. In many hundreds of cases, merchants, manufacturers, and other employers, have voluntarily paid the salaries or wages of their clerks or employés, who have volunteered, to their families during their period of service in the army.

race, was there a rebellion so utterly unjustifiable in its character; or which, aiming at the subversion of a benign Government, only that it might rear upon its ruins, a despotism, having Slavery for its corner-stone, was so well calculated to call forth the scorn and abhorrence of all good and honorable men.

Postscript.—The delay which has occurred in the publication of this pamphlet, enables the writer to add a few items of additional evidence of the generous responses made by our people for the relief of those who are sufferers from the war. The Sanitary Commission has received for aid to the sick and wounded of the battles around Gettysburg, and the wounded at Vicksburg (rebel as well as Union soldiers), over $50,000 in money and large amounts of supplies; the Christian Commission over $30,000 in money and abundant supplies; and other organizations, not less than $100,000 in money and supplies. Since the riot in New York, which was prompted by sympathy with the Rebellion, nearly $55,000 have been contributed for the soldiers and policemen wounded, and the families of those killed by the rioters, and about $35,000, beside large amounts of clothing for the colored sufferers from the riot.

STATISTICAL TABLES.

Note.—In the following Statistical Tables it has been necessary, in some instances, to estimate the amounts contributed by small societies, individuals, &c., in the aggregate. Wherever this has been necessary, it has only been done after the most careful inquiry and investigation, and a comparison of the views of cautious and well-informed persons, and the lowest estimate has invariably been taken. It is believed, therefore, that the amounts are, in nearly every case, below the actual sums contributed.

Tabular Statement of the Contributions for various purposes connected, directly or indirectly, with the War.

		AGGREGATE.
I.—Amount expended by the States for the equipment and maintenance of troops, not reimbursed or guaranteed to be reimbursed by the General Government :		
Maine..............................	$40,000 00	
New Hampshire (estimated)............	60,000 00	
Vermont.............................	75,000 00	
Massachusetts........................	1,963,311 88	
Rhode Island.........................	598,286 04	
Connecticut..........................	1,610,900 94	
New York............................	3,340,943 00	
New Jersey..........................	251,320 03	
Pennsylvania........................	1,448,000 00	
Ohio (estimated).....................	1,600,000 00	
Wisconsin...........................	250,000 00	
Kansas..............................	40,000 00	
		$11,277,761 89
II.—Bounties, extra pay, and allowance to families of volunteers made by States :		
Maine	$2,750,000 00	
New Hampshire (estimated)............	519,000 00	
Vermont.............................	1,125,000 00	
Massachusetts	2,620,000 00	
Rhode Island........................	1,422,888 00	
Connecticut	1,857,044 00	
New York...........................	5,410,750 00	
New Jersey (estimated)...............	1,500,000 00	
Ohio (estimated).....................	2,300,000 00	
Michigan............................	1,400,000 00	
Wisconsin...........................	720,000 00	
		21,624,672 00
Carried forward................		$32,902,433 89

		AGGREGATE.
Brought forward................	....	$32,902,433 89
III.—Moneys contributed by cities, towns, corporations, and individuals, for raising and recruiting regiments :		
At the beginning of the war............	$7,120,000 00	
In the summer and autumn of 1862......	16,150,000 00	
Philadelphia, in June and July, 1863.....	1,000,000 00	
Other cities, at the same time...........	150,000 00	
		24,420,000 00
IV.—Bounties and aid to families of volunteers contributed by counties, towns, cities, corporations, and individuals in each State :		
Maine..................................	$420,000 00	
New Hampshire (estimated)............	660,000 00	
Vermont..............................	820,000 00	
Massachusetts	1,815,285 30	
Rhode Island..........................	937,264 38	
Connecticut	1,746,360 00	
New York.............................	16,800,000 00	
New Jersey (estimated).................	2,250,000 00	
Pennsylvania..........................	7,200,000 00	
Delaware.............................	60,000 00	
Maryland	800,000 00	
Ohio (estimated)......................	6,300,000 00	
Indiana (estimated)...................	1,428,000 00	
Illinois...............................	1,065,000 00	
Michigan..............................	685,000 00	
Wisconsin.............................	1,750,000 00	
Iowa (estimated)......................	800,000 00	
Minnesota (estimated).................	150,000 00	
Missouri (estimated)..................	300,000 00	
Kansas................................	100,000 00	
		46,086,909 68
V.—State contributions for sick and wounded soldiers, Governor's contingent fund or special appropriations :		
Maine................................	$25,000 00	
Vermont..............................	10,000 00	
Massachusetts	25,400 00	
Connecticut	28,641 00	
New York.............................	250,000 00	
Maryland..............................	10,000 00	
Illinois...............................	59,000 00	
Michigan..............................	48,000 00	
Wisconsin.............................	40,000 00	
Iowa (estimated)......................	50,000 00	
Minnesota (estimated).................	20,000 00	
Missouri	50,000 00	
		616,041 00
VI.—Contributions of States to National Defense not included under any of the foregoing heads :		
Maine for harbor defenses.............	$200,000 00	
Carried forward...............	$200,000 00	$104,025,384 57

		AGGREGATE.
Brought forward...............	$200,000 00	$104,025,394 57
Massachusetts for harbor and coast defenses and State war vessels..........	1,500,000 00	
New York for harbor defenses, &c.......	1,000,000 00	
Pennsylvania for harbor defense and protection from invasions.................	2,500,000 00	
Ohio for protection of river line.........	1,500,000 00	
Kentucky for Home Guards, &c...........	1,000,000 00	
Missouri for Home Guards..............	1,000,000 00	
Maryland for Home Guards, &c..........	400,000 00	
		$9,100,000 00
Total contributions from the States, counties, &c., for aid and relief of soldiers and their families, and for purposes of national defense, not reimbursed or to be reimbursed by the General Government................................		$113,125,394 57
VII.—Contributions for the care and comfort of soldiers, whether in camp, or sick or wounded, and for their families, from associations and individuals :		
U. S. Sanitary Commission, in money....	$795,174 09	
U. S. Sanitary Commission, supplies, estimated value.........................	2,755,097 24	
Western Sanitary Commission, in money.	151,138 18	
Western Sanitary Commission, supplies, estimated value........................	395,335 96	
Chicago Sanitary Commission, in money..	42,714 00	
" " " in supplies.	300,000 00	
Philadelphia Branch of Sanitary Commission, not included in United States Sanitary Commission....................	71,000 00	
Iowa Sanitary Commission, money and supplies.............................	58,400 00	
Indiana State Sanitary Commission, money and supplies....................	100,000 00	
U. S. Christian Commission, in money...	120,000 00	
" " " in supplies..	400,000 00	
New England Soldiers' Relief Association, money..............................	20,000 00	
New England Soldiers' Relief Association, supplies.............................	150,000 00	
Ladies' Aid Society of Philadelphia, money	13,791 17	
" " " supplies	200,000 00	
Soldiers' Aid Society of Hartford, Ct., money.............................	12,000 00	
Soldiers' Aid Society of Hartford, Ct., supplies.............................	30,000 00	
Union Relief Association of Baltimore, and other Baltimore Associations, in money.	60 000 00	
Union Relief Association of Baltimore, and other Baltimore Associations, in supplies	125,000 00	
State Relief Associations at Washington, money and supplies..................	1,030,000 00	
Carried forward................	$6,829,650 64	

	AGGREGATE.
Brought forward..............	$6,829,650 64	
Other Relief Associations, not connected with the national organizations, East and West (estimated)................	1,500,000 00	
Union Volunteer Refreshment Saloon, Philadelphia, cash..............	34,738 86	
Union Volunteer Refreshment Saloon, Philadelphia, supplies................	60,000 00	
Cooper Shop Refreshment Saloon, cash, about............................	30,000 00	
Cooper Shop Refreshment Saloon, supplies................................	70,000 00	
Citizens' Volunteer Hospital, Philadelphia, money, labor, and supplies............	55,000 00	
Soldiers' homes, restaurants, &c. (not connected with the Sanitary Commissions), in all the principal cities, about forty in all.................................	250,000 00	
American Bible Society and its auxiliaries, Bibles distributed to soldiers...	120,000 00	
American Tract Society, New York, for books and tracts distributed to soldiers, and services of missionaries and colporteurs	60,000 00	
American Tract Society, Boston, do......	63,000 00	
Other religious societies, missionaries, and publications........................	35,000 00	
Supplies and money distributed to armies in Virginia and hospitals in Washington and vicinity, through individuals......	1,200,000 00	
Money for postage, stationery, and supplies, distributed to ninety hospitals east of the Alleghanies (estimated)........	800,000 00	
Supplies and money forwarded to western armies and hospitals directly from towns, cities, and villages, and not passing through other organizations (estimated)	5,000,000 00	
Ambulances for sick and wounded, built and maintained by Philadelphia firemen	20,600 00	
Asylums and homes for disabled soldiers and for children of deceased soldiers, in New York and elsewhere............:..	80,000 00	
Young Men's Christian Associations, aside from contributions through Christian Commissions..........	128,000 00	
Board of Trade, Chicago, for "Board of Trade regiments"....................	65,000 00	
H. M. Pierce, LL.D., in efforts for relief of soldiers, and attempt to secure organization of ambulance corps...........	1,000 00	
Col. J. H. Almy, A. Q. M. G., agent for Connecticut and Rhode Island, at New York	1,600 00	
Col. F. E. Howe, C. W. Burton, D. E. Clark, and other State agents, for soldiers in New York not less than.......	5,000 00	$16,408,589 50

		AGGREGATE.
VIII.—CONTRIBUTIONS FOR SUFFERERS ABROAD.		
International Relief Fund, New York, for Lancashire sufferers...................	$125,000 00	
Corn Exchange Fund, for Lancashire sufferers...............................	50,000 00	
Philadelphia contributions..............	90,000 00	
Relief of French operatives..............	8,000 00	
Ship-load of provisions for Irish sufferers, contributed by A. T. Stewart, New York	30,000 00	
Contributions for Irish Relief in N. York..	30,000 00	
" " " in Brooklyn.	15,000 00	
" " " elsewhere...	35,000 00	
		$383,000 00
IX.—CONTRIBUTIONS FOR FREEDMEN.		
Freedman's Aid Society, New York, money and supplies..................	$175,000 00	
Freedman's Aid Societies in other cities...	200,000 00	
Aid to Freedmen by missionary societies, &c.................................	25,000 00	
		$400,000 00
X.—SOLDIERS' ALLOTMENTS TO THEIR FAMILIES.		
In New York..........................	$6,341,000 00	
In other States........................	9,750,000 00	
		$16,091,000 00
XI.—Advances made by the States to the General Government, for which they claim, but have not yet received, reimbursement...............	$25,701,991 00	

Appendix A.

THE UNITED STATES SANITARY COMMISSION.

This organization, which has exerted so great an influence for good on the Army, originated from three previously existing associations in New York city, viz. : "The Woman's Central Association of Relief for the Sick and Wounded of the Army ;" " The Advisory Committee of the Board of Physicians and Surgeons of the Hospitals of New York," and the New York Medical Association for furnishing Medical Supplies in aid of the Army."

On the 18th of May, 1861, Messrs. Henry W. Bellows, D. D., W. H. Van Buren, M. D., Elisha Harris, M. D., and Jacob Harsen, M. D., representatives of these three associations, drew up and forwarded to the Secretary of War a communication setting forth the propriety of creating an organization which should unite the duties and labors of the three associations, and co-operate with the Medical Bureau of the War Department to such an extent that each might aid the other in securing the welfare of the Army. For this purpose they asked that a mixed commission of civilians, military officers, and medical men, might be appointed by the Government, charged with the duty of methodizing and reducing to practical service the already active but undirected benevolence of the people toward the army, who should consider the general subject of the prevention of sickness and suffering among the troops, and suggest the wisest method which the people at large could use to manifest their good-will toward the comfort, security, and health of the army. They referred to the Commissions which followed the Crimean and Indian wars, and brought to light the vast amount of suffering which had been needlessly endured there, and begged that, in this case, the organization might *precede* the war, and prevent so far as possible the suffering which would otherwise ensue. They suggested, also, the appointment of cooks and nurses for the army, and stated that the "Woman's Central Association of Relief" stood ready to undertake the training of both in their duties.

On the 22d of May, R. C. Wood, M. D., then Acting Surgeon-General, now in charge of the Western Medical Department, followed this communication by a letter addressed to the Secretary of War, urging the establishment of the desired Commission as a needed adjunct to the new, extensive, and overwhelming duties of the Medical Bureau.

After a hearing of the representatives of the New York Associations, the Secretary of War, on the 9th of June, decided on the creation of such a Commission, the President approving. The title first given to the new organization was " The Commission of Inquiry and Advice in respect of the Sanitary Interests of the United States Forces," but was subsequently changed to " The United States Sanitary Commission."

It was composed of the following gentlemen : Rev. Henry W. Bellows, D. D., President, New York ; Prof. A. D. Bache, Vice-President, Washington ; Elisha Harris, M. D., Corresponding Secretary, New York ; George W. Cullum, U. S. A., Washington ; Alexander E. Shiras, U. S. A., Washington ; Robert C. Wood, M. D., U. S. A., Washington ; William H. Van Buren, M. D., New York ; Wolcott Gibbs, M. D., New York ; Cornelius R. Agnew, M. D., New York ; George T. Strong, New York ; Frederick Law Olmsted, New York ; Samuel G. Howe, M. D., Boston ; J. S. Newberry, M. D., Cleveland, Ohio. To these were subsequently added Horace Binney, Jr., Philadelphia ; Rt. Rev. Thomas M. Clark, D. D., Providence, R. I. ; Hon. Joseph Holt, Kentucky ; R. W. Burnett, Cincinnati, Ohio ; Hon. Mark Skinner, Chicago, Ill., and about four hundred associate members, in all parts of the country.

The Commission proceeded at once to organize its action and to appoint committees from its members to visit every camp, recruiting-post, transport, fort, hospital, and military station, to ascertain and report all abuses, and to perfect such organizations as might insure a higher degree of health and comfort for the soldiers.

The medical members of the Commission undertook to consider the questions which might arise concerning the diseases of the camp, and their medical and surgical treatment, from the highest scientific point of view, and guided by the rich and abundant experience of European army surgeons.

Three important committees were appointed, one to communicate the matured counsels of the Commission to the Government, and procure their ordering by the proper Departments ; a second to maintain a direct relation with the army officers and medical men, with the camps and hospitals, and by all proper methods to make sure of the carrying out of the sanitary orders of the Medical Bureau and the War Department ; and a third to be in constant communication with the State Governments, and the public benevolent associations interested in the army.

This plan of organization was approved by the Secretary of War, on the 13th of June, 1861, and on the 21st of that month the Commission issued its first address to the public. This was soon followed by an eloquent appeal to the Life Insurance Companies, and another to men of wealth throughout the country for aid in the prosecution of its work. The members of the Commission, as such, received no compensation, but the purposes of the organization would require a very considerable number of paid employés, and would involve heavy expenses for publications and supplies, which could only be purchased with money. A considerable number of associate members were elected at this time, who gave their services in raising means for the operations of the Commission, and Ladies' Associations, in all parts of the country, prepared clothing and supplies of all sorts, and forwarded them to its depots.

The members of the Commission visited, during the summer of 1861, the different camps of the widely-extended armies of the Republic, and carefully inspected and reported upon their sanitary condition and needs.

As time rolled on, and the number of soldiers greatly increased, and especially as severe battles occurred, and malaria visited the camps, the duties and responsibilities of the Commission to the sick and wounded greatly increased, and their means of supplying the wants of the scores of thousands, who looked to them for such aid as the Medical Bureau of the Government could not give, were augmented in an equally rapid ratio.

Its Medical Inspectors, who were scientific experts, accompanied every column of the army, and, by advice, direction, and if necessary by complaint, regulated the sanitary condition of the men to the best degree possible. Supplies were sent by the Commission with every expedition, entirely supplementary to those of the Departments at Washington, and derived from the donations of the public. Whenever there were sick or wounded soldiers, there was found a trustworthy agent of the Sanitary Commission, ready to supply them with medical treatment, food, clothing, or transportation, as the case might require.

On the battle-field they hovered round, fearless of danger to themselves, only seeking to alleviate pain in others. Thousands of soldiers, sick, wounded, convalescent, discharged, weekly received its shelter and its food ; its safe conduct, its transportation facilities, its aid in securing their pay and pensions. Every military hospital in the country was subject to the visitations of its medical agents, and every defect and short-coming was reported to the Surgeon-General, and at once remedied as far as possible.

By means of a registration plan, every sick or wounded soldier known to any Department of the Government, could be traced directly to his present locality, on application to the Sanitary Commission.

It has, throughout, worked in harmony with the United States Government, and especially with the Medical Bureau, to which it has proved of great service. That Bureau, which, at the commencement of the war, was utterly inadequate, though from no fault of its own, to the vast work before it, is now well regulated and admirably organized, having a corps of three thousand skillful and responsible surgeons, and fifteen thousand hired nurses experienced in their duties.

The weeding out from this force of the ignorant, unskillful, and incompetent, and the training of those now in the service to their duties, has been largely aided by the direct personal efforts, and the professional publications of the medical members of the Commission ; and this brings us to say that one sphere of usefulness peculiar to the Sanitary Commission, has been the publication and circulation among the Surgeons in the Army, of monograms upon medical subjects of the greatest interest, in connection with their field of operations. These monograms are prepared, by the most competent men, with special reference to the condition of our army, and form a little circulating library of just such material as is most required.

Among these publications are, a " Report of a Committee on the use of Quinine as a prophylactic against Malarious Diseases ;" Directions to Army Surgeons on the Field of Battle ;" " Report of a Committee on the value of Vaccination in Armies ;" " Report of a Committee on the subject of Amputation ;" " Report of a Committee on the subject of Venereal Diseases ;" " Report of a Committee on the subject of Pneumonia ;" " Report of a Committee on the subject of Continued Fevers ;" Report of a Committee on Dysentery ;" " Report of a Committee on the subject of Scurvy ;" with others, on the treatment of "Fractures," " Miasmatic Fevers," " Yellow Fever," &c., &c. Then there are " Instructions for Camp Inspectors ;" " Rules for Preserving the Health of the Soldier," and others more practical in their nature, and interesting to any one interested in the Army.

Perhaps one among the most kindly and humane labors of the Commission has been the establishment in Washington of the " Home," a depot where the soldier, honorably discharged on account of wounds, sickness, or physical disability, could receive aid to enable him to proceed directly to his home and friends, being fed, comfortably clothed and housed, his necessary papers procured for him by an efficient agent, and himself kept from the temptations of the city, until furnished with a through ticket, he was put on the cars and started for his own town ; this, which has been termed the " Special Relief" service, has been most admirably and effectively conducted.

As an illustration of the working of the system, we will give a few statistics from September 10, 1861, to December 15, 1862 :

Number of soldiers received at the "Home,"...... 14,106
Number of nights' lodging furnished.............. 36,866
Number of meals furnished 81,769
Cost of the " Home " to the Commission during the
    above period............................... $11,030

The " Lodge," an establishment supplementary to the "Home," was built in December last. It is located directly opposite to the Paymaster's office, in order to give rest and food to the invalid soldier while waiting for his pay, and to prevent his falling into the hands of the harpies, who would plunder him of his hard earned wages. Its uses are best seen by reading the following " ticket," a copy of which is given to every discharged soldier on his appearance at the office of the Paymaster :

"The bearer, ———, an invalid soldier, will find a resting place and food, without charge, at the Lodge No. 3, of the Sanitary Commission, No. 210 F. street, opposite Paymaster's office."

During the first two weeks after this place was opened, over two hundred and fifty meals, and forty lodgings *per diem*, were furnished, according to the ticket. A table was kept constantly spread for fifty persons, and the one hundred and fifty or two hundred lame and sick soldiers that formerly thronged the streets were supplied with all necessary comforts, preparatory to the more laborious task of setting their faces homeward.

To the enabling soldiers to obtain their discharge papers and their pay, the Commission has paid particular attention, having special agents in charge of this duty.

After the battle of Antietam, the Commission expended $20,000, in a few days, for comforts, assistance, and medicine to the wounded. As a further illustration of the character of the labors of the Sanitary Commission, we will refer to the battle of Fredericksburg, which may be taken as a sample of their usual course at such times.

The Commission received the report of the battle on the evening of December 13, the day on which it occurred. On the following morning a propeller was laden with stores, and with twelve special agents of the Commission, chiefly medical men, started for the scene of action. Eleven of the regular agents were also with the army at the same time. On this occasion there were delivered to the soldiers from the stores of the Commission, 1,800 blankets, 900 quilts, 5,642 woolen shirts, 4,139 pairs woolen drawers, 4,269 pairs socks, 2,500 towels, 16 barrels dried fruit, 10 boxes soda biscuit, 6 barrels crackers, 1,000 pounds concentrated milk. Beside these a kitchen was improvised, and good food, well cooked, was served out to the sick and wounded soldiers.

The Commission had received, up to the 1st of June, 1863, $795,174.09 in money, besides $172,000 contributed to co-operating local Commissions, and $2,755,097.24 in supplies, aside from over $400,000 in supplies distributed independent of it, by co-operating organizations, making a grand total of $4,120,000 contributed to this single organization and its auxiliaries. Since June 1, to July 15, it has received not less than $75,000 in money, and over $100,000 in supplies.

6

Appendix B.

The Western Sanitary Commission derived its first authority from the following order of Major-General Fremont :

HEADQUARTERS, WESTERN DEPARTMENT,
St. Louis, Mo. Sept. 5, 1861.

SPECIAL ORDERS, No. 159.

With a view to the health and comfort of the Volunteer troops in and near to the city of St. Louis, a Sanitary Commission is hereby appointed, to consist of five gentlemen, who shall serve voluntarily, and be removable at pleasure. Its general object shall be to carry out, under the properly-constituted military authorities, and in compliance with their orders, such sanitary regulations and reforms as the well-being of the soldiers demand.

The Commission shall have authority—*under the directions of the Medical Director,* to select, fit up, and furnish suitable buildings for Army and Brigade Hospitals, in such place, and in such manner as circumstances require. It will attend to the selection and appointment of women nurses, under the authority and by the direction of Miss D. L. Dix, General Superintendent of the nurses of Military Hospitals in the United States. It will co-operate with the Surgeons of the several hospitals in providing male nurses, and in whatever manner practicable, and by their consent. It shall have authority to visit the different camps, to consult with the commanding officers, and the Colonels and other officers of the several regiments, with regard to the sanitary and general condition of the troops, and aid them in providing proper means for the preservation of health and prevention of sickness, by supplies of wholesome and well-cooked food, by good systems of drainage, and other practicable methods. It will obtain from the community at large such additional means of increasing the comfort and promoting the moral and social welfare of the men, in camp and hospital, as may be needed, and cannot be furnished by Government regulations. It will, from time to time, report directly to the Commander-in-chief of the department, the condition of the camps and hospitals, with such suggestions as can properly be made by a Sanitary Board.

This Commission is not intended in any way to interfere with the Medical Staff, or other officers of the Army, but to co-operate with them, and aid them in the discharge of their present arduous and extraordinary duties. It will be treated by all officers of the Army, both regular and volunteer, in this Department, with the respect due to the humane and patriotic motives of the members, and to the authority of the Commander-in-chief.

This Sanitary Commission will, for the present, consist of Jas. E. Yeatman, Esq.; C. S. Greeley, Esq.; J. B. Johnson, M.D.; George Partridge, Esq.; and the Rev. William G. Eliot, D. D.

By order of Major-General J. C. FREMONT.

J. C. KELTON,
Assistant Adjutant-General.

The authority conferred by this order was recognized and confirmed by Major-General Halleck, who added Dr. S. Pollak to the Commission, and still later, viz., December 16, 1862, by an order from the Secretary of War (Hon. E. M. Stanton), extending the field of its labors, and reappointing the members of the Commission as at first constituted.

This Commission has not devoted its attention to as wide a range of topics as the United States Sanitary Commission, but has confined itself to the work of superintending hospitals, furnishing supplies, appointing nurses, visiting and caring for the sick and wounded of the Army of the Southwest Frontier, the District of East Arkansas, the armies operating on both sides of the Mississippi, and the Mississippi Naval Flotilla; it has at all times acted in concert with the Medical Directors and inspectors of these armies, and on account of their efficient supervision of the condition and sanitary wants of the armies under their charge, has not found it necessary to appoint separate medical inspectors. It has the superintendence of twelve hospitals (one for officers and another for military prisoners), having accommodations for about eight thousand patients, besides ten large hospital steamers and floating hospitals ; it has established Soldiers' Homes, and Soldiers' Lodges, at St. Louis, Memphis, and Columbus, Ky., and agencies at Helena, Milliken's Bend, and Springfield, Mo., and has prepared, published and distributed, a large edition of a "Treatise on the Preservation of the Health of the Soldier, the cooking of food, the preparation of diet for the sick, the duties of nurses and attendants, and the organization and general management of Hospitals." It has also kept a registry of the location and condition of invalid and wounded soldiers in the Western armies.

The Commission has received to June 1, 1863, cash donations to the amount of $151,381.18, and sanitary stores and supplies of the estimated value of $395,335.96, making a total of $546,716.14. The expenses incurred in the collection and distribution of this large amount were only $8,848.86, or 1½ per cent. of the entire amount received and distributed.

Appendix C.

From the commencement of the war the Young Men's Christian Associations, in most of the larger cities and towns of the loyal States, had contributed largely, not only in money and supplies, to the relief and comfort of the soldiers, but in personal service. Many of their members were in the army, and the sympathy felt for them by those who remained at home prompted to efficient action for the spiritual as well as physical needs of the army. After every considerable battle, members of these associations were dispatched with money, sanitary stores and supplies, and religious and moral reading matter for free distribution to the sufferers. One Young Men's Christian Association, that of Brooklyn, N. Y., had contributed in this way more than $28,000 for this purpose, and had given in addition the voluntary services of several of its members in distributing supplies and caring for the sick and wounded on the battle-fields of the East and the West. Others had done nearly as much, some, perhaps, even more.

At a convention of these Christian Associations, held in New York November 16, 1861, it was resolved to organize from the representatives of these bodies a United States Christian Commission, and the following persons were appointed : Rev. Rollin H. Neale, D. D., Boston ; George H. Stuart, Esq., Philadelphia ; Rev. Bishop E. S. Janes, D. D., New York ; Rev. M. L. R. P. Thompson, D. D., Cincinnati ; Hon. Benjamin F. Manierre, New York ; Colonel Clinton B. Fisk, St. Louis ; Rev. Benjamin C. Cutler, D. D., Brooklyn ; John V. Farwell, Esq., Chicago ; Mitchell H. Miller, Esq., Washington ; John D. Hill, M. D., Buffalo. During the succeeding year Mr. Manierre and Rev. Dr. Cutler resigned, and their places were filled by the appointment of Jay Cooke, Esq., of Philadelphia, and Rev. James Eells, D. D., of Brooklyn.

Soon after its appointment the Commission met in Washington, and organized by choosing George H. Stuart, of Philadelphia, Chairman, and B. F. Manierre, of New York, Secretary and Treasurer. Its headquarters were at first established in New York, and Rev. A. M. Morrison was appointed Secretary, when it was ascertained that the labors of the two offices would be too much for one man. Mr. Morrison's services were rendered gratuitously. Some months were occupied in the organization of branches, in obtaining from Government and from railroad and telegraph lines, passes, and in adjusting the details for the vast work which soon began to flow in upon them, and it was not till the summer of 1862 that the Commission was fairly ready for its work ; meantime its headquarters had been removed to Philadelphia, and Rev. William E. Boardman appointed Secretary in place of Rev. Mr. Morrison, resigned.

Its objects, as declared in its circulars, were " to arouse the Christian Associations and the Christian men and women of the loyal States to such action toward the men in our army and navy as would be pleasing to the Master ; to obtain and direct volunteer labors, and to collect stores and money with which to supply whatever is needed, reading matter and articles necessary for health, not furnished by Government or other agencies, and to give the officers and men of our army and navy the best Christian ministries, for both body and soul, possible in their circumstances."

The Commission is organized upon the principle of voluntary, unpaid agency. Its Chairman, a merchant of Philadelphia, not only devotes almost his entire time to its service, but furnishes office-room and storage, clerks, porters, &c., to conduct the business correspondence and pack the stores and supplies, free of charge. The railroad companies have uniformly given free passes to its delegates, and the telegraph companies free transmission to its messages. It has been largely aided by grants of Bibles, religious books, tracts, &c., from the Bible and publishing societies, and donations of newspapers, religious and secular, from the publishers of those papers ; its delegates are volunteers, whose expenses of living are alone furnished by the Commission, and who spend some weeks or months in ministrations of kindness to the sick and wounded ; it has also employed a very large corps of volunteer chaplains to visit the regiments and brigades of the army, and manifest their sympathy with the soldier, and seek to improve his physical and moral condition.

It has commissioned for this work more than six hundred delegates, lay and clerical, has disbursed for expenses and purchases of stores about $120,000, and distributed stores and supplies to the amount of $400,000 more, aside from the gifts of free passes and telegrams by railroad and telegraph companies, which would amount to nearly, or quite, $100,000.

About 150,000 Bibles and Testaments, and as many volumes of other works, generally of a religious character, have been distributed by its delegates, besides 12,000,000 pages of tracts, over 450,000 newspapers, 150,000 hymn books, 350,000 temperance documents, and 40,000 to 50,000 magazines and periodicals.

Appendix D.

BIBLE, TRACT, AND PUBLICATION SOCIETIES.

Though none of these were originated by the war, they have, without exception, made large grants of their publications, and those of them which employ colporteurs or delegates have sent to the army earnest and efficient workers to minister to the physical as well as the spiritual wants of the soldier. The American Bible Society has, either by direct grant or through its auxiliaries, furnished either a Bible or a Testament to all of our soldiers who would accept it; and has also furnished large numbers to the rebel prisoners, and to the rebel army. The two National Tract Societies have made large grants of their publications, and have sent colporteurs or missionaries into the field to visit the hospitals and regiments, and see to the proper distribution of their books; and the American Sunday School Union, the Episcopal Tract and Book Societies, the Presbyterian Publication Board and Publication Committee, the Reformed Dutch Board of Publication, the American Baptist Publication Society, the American and Foreign Bible Society, and the Methodist Book Concern, have all contributed largely to swell the amount of religious reading in the army. The cost of books thus distributed does not fall below $300,000.

Appendix E.

With some exceptions, the efforts of these societies have been addressed to the evangelization and spiritual oversight of the freedmen, or, as they are popularly called, "contrabands."

A very considerable number of the missionaries of the American Home Missionary Society, the American Baptist Home Mission Society, the Presbyterian Board of Domestic Missions, and other similar organizations, have become chaplains in the army or hospitals, or delegates of the Christian Commission, and have performed valuable and efficient service in these capacities. In a few instances they have been sent to occupy fields to which before the war, there was no admission in consequence of the opposition of slaveholders, as, for instance, in Missouri, Wester, Virginia, and Tennessee.

The American Missionary Association, the American Baptist Free Mission Society, the American Baptist Home Mission Society, and, perhaps, some other organizations, have commissioned missionaries to labor among the freedmen at Washington, Fortress Monroe, Port Royal, and Helena, Arkansas. In some instances, these missionaries have also ministered to the sick and wounded soldiers. The aggregate expenditure of these societies for missionary labor among the freedmen and soldiers is about $50,000.

7

Appendix F.

The number of these it is impossible to estimate. There are few cities or towns of considerable size, few villages even, in which there is not at least one of them, which collects money, and prepares clothing, hospital stores, and hospital furniture for the army.

In the cities there is usually one to each church, and sometimes a larger one to which the lesser are auxiliaries. Many of these send their collections of money and supplies, directly or indirectly (through the Women's Central Association of Relief), to the United States Sanitary Commission; some (at the West) send to the Western Sanitary Commission; some to the Christian Commission; a considerable number to the New England Soldiers' Relief; or to the State Relief organizations at Washington, St. Louis, and elsewhere; or to individuals who will distribute their supplies; while some have their own agents in the field, or at Washington, Louisville, Nashville, Memphis, &c., and distribute their bounty through them.

The Women's Central Association of Relief, No. 10 Cooper Union, New York, though now a branch of the United States Sanitary Commission, antedates that body in its organization. It was formally organized on the 29th of April, 1861, and combined in itself several other associations which had been projected for the same purpose, that of energizing and concentrating the efforts of the women all over the country, who were desirous of doing something for the army, either in the contribution and preparation of clothing, hospital furniture and stores, or of serving as nurses and assistants in the hospitals, &c. It has collected about $30,000 in money, and a vast amount of stores, clothing, &c., all of which have been handed over to the Sanitary Commission. It was as representative members of this Association that

Rev. Dr. Bellows and Dr. E. Harris united with Drs. Van Buren and Harsen, representing other organizations, in that memorial to the Secretary of War which led to the creation of the Sanitary Commission.

The "Ladies' Aid Society of Philadelphia" is an independent organization, of even earlier date than the "Women's Central Association of Relief." It was founded on the 26th of April, 1861, only eleven days after the President's first proclamation, and has proved a most effective helper in the care of the sick and wounded soldier. The secretary of the Society, Mrs. John Harris, a lady of the highest respectability and social position, has superintended in person the distribution of the supplies furnished by the Society, spending many months with the army, and preparing food and clothing, and nursing the sick and wounded with as assiduous care as the most tender and loving mother could have done.

She has been to the Army of the Potomac what Florence Nightingale and her coadjutors were to the English army in the Crimean war. Yet it would be wrong to bestow this meed of praise on her alone, for though few have done more than she, there are others who have done nearly as much. Many, whose own hearts have been sorely smitten by the casualties of the war, like the widow of Major-General Richardson in the Army of the Potomac, the widow of General Lander, in the Army of the South, and the widows of General W. H. L. Wallace and of Governor Louis P. Harvey, in the Army of the Mississippi, have found consolation for their own sorrows in ministering to the wounded and dying of the army. Mothers, whose sons have fallen on the battle-field, have sought to do a mother's duty to those who lay at death's door, from wounds or sickness, without a mother to comfort them ; and sisters, bereft of a brother's love and care, have sought by deeds of kindness to others, to alleviate the anguish of the wounds, which the war had brought to their own hearts.

But to return to the Ladies' Society. Its disbursements had been about $40,000 in money, and over $200,000 in supplies, previous to recent battles of the first days of July.

There are many more of these Ladies' Aid Societies, which are deserving of especial mention, such as those of Hartford, Connecticut ; Cleveland, Ohio ; Peoria, Illinois ; Cincinnati, Chicago,

Indianapolis, Louisville and St. Louis. All of them have been abundant in good works, and several of them have acted independently of any other association or commission ; but more of them were organized quite as early as the two we have named.

Appendix G.

These are generally composed of persons of both sexes, and have usually had for their object the special assistance of the sick, wounded, disabled, furloughed, or discharged soldiers of some particular State or States. One of the most efficient of these has been the New England Soldiers' Relief Association, founded by sons of New England, resident in New York, April 3, 1862. It has not confined its benefactions to New England soldiers, but has aided and cared for the sick and wounded soldiers from all the States, when passing through New York. It has thus relieved over twenty thousand soldiers, furnishing meals, lodging, hospital attendance, and service in obtaining back pay, pensions, and discharges, and in preventing the frauds so constantly attempted to be practised on the soldier by the designing and unprincipled. Its expenditures in money have been about $20,000, and it has received and disbursed large quantities of supplies, but of these we cannot ascertain the exact amount. Its lady members have undertaken to furnish from their own number a corps of nurses, who have attended regularly in their turns, to minister to the sick and wounded, and a voluntary corps of night watchers was organized from the gentlemen.

The Union Relief Association, of Baltimore, is another very efficient organization, just now (July, 1863) overwhelmed with the care of a vast number of the wounded from the battles around Gettysburg. It originated from the benevolent impulses of the loyal citizens of that city, who had seen with bitter indignation, its fair fame disgraced by the cowardly mob who attacked the Massachusetts Sixth Regiment, on the 19th of April, 1861, and the subsequent high-handed abetting of treason by some of its prominent citizens. It was organized on the 28th of June, 1861, and has been remarkable for the intensity of its loyalty, and its earnest effort to render every aid and comfort in its power to Union soldiers. Similar organizations exist in most of the large cities of the country.

Appendix H.

Under a variety of names, these places, where food, and, if necessary, lodging, and in some cases temporary hospital attendance, are furnished gratuitously to soldiers, either in squads or regiments, are becoming numerous.

Some, like the Soldiers' Rest, in New York, or the Park Barracks formerly, are established by State or city authorities ; others by the United States Sanitary Commission, like the Soldiers' Home and Soldiers' Lodges, at Washington and at Aquia creek ; others, by the Western Sanitary Commission, as at St. Louis, Memphis, and Columbus, Kentucky, while a number are the results of the spontaneous benevolence of citizens in the vicinities where the soldiers pass in the largest numbers, Among the most remarkable of these are the "Union Volunteer Refreshment Saloon" and the "Cooper Shop Refreshment Saloon," in Philadelphia. The origin of the first named was as follows : When the three-months' men commenced passing through the city, there were no arrangements for feeding them, nor for taking care of the sick. The citizens living upon the streets between the landing and the depot gave the soldiers water, tea, and coffee, and often more substantial nourishment, but being hard-working people, they could ill afford even so limited benevolence. At length Bazilla S. Brown gave notice that he would receive and dispense at a convenient place upon the sidewalk whatever articles of food his friends might see proper to contribute. He commenced his labor of love, with eleven pounds of coffee, upon a curbstone, and from that simple beginning of a poor but good man, this benevolent institution took its rise. The necessity for concerted action was soon apparent, and the Union Volunteer Refreshment Committee was accordingly organized on the 27th of

May, 1861. The following is a copy of the first notice by telegraph of the expected arrival of a regiment :

OFFICE OF CAMDEN AND AMBOY }
R. R. TRANSPORTATION CO. }

PHILADELPHIA, MAY 27, 1861.

B. S. BROWN, DEAR SIR—We have a dispatch from New York stating that the Eighth New York Regiment leave New York to-day, and will arrive here about 3, A. M. About eight hundred men in the regiment.

Yours, truly,

(Signed.)   E. J. BURROWS.

The Committee procured a small building (formerly a boat shop and riggers' loft), situated near the southwest corner of Washington and Swanson streets, and have gradually increased its dimensions, until the main saloon covers a lot of ground 95 by 150 feet, and twelve hundred men can now be accommodated at a time at the tables, while the most ample facilities are furnished for washing, bathing, and writing letters. By these means nearly three hundred thousand soldiers have been received, entertained, and provided for, since the commencement of the war. Two hospitals are attached to the institution, containing at present fifty beds, for the use of the soldiers, or those who have been soldiers, who break down on their journey, or are too much enfeebled to proceed at once to their homes, and would otherwise have been thrown helpless, among strangers.

The "Cooper Shop Refreshment Saloon" originated about the same time and from similar circumstances. It is at 1109 Otsego street, but a short distance from the Union Saloon, and, though not quite so large, has had a growth and career very much like its neighbor. Both are liberally sustained by the citizens of Philadelphia, and no regiment or company of soldiers passes through Philadelphia, either going to, or returning from, the seat of war, without experiencing the hospitality and kind attentions of one or other of these institutions. The receipts of the two in money and supplies have been somewhat more than $200,000

Appendix I.

At the time when the earlier great battles of the War created a demand for hospital accommodations for scores of thousands of the sick and wounded, the Government, though it had made what provision it could for the emergency, was but poorly provided with hospitals, well and properly furnished, and was compelled to call upon the civil hospitals of the large cities to receive large numbers of patients who needed immediate care, and could not await the erection of temporary hospitals.

In this way, in the autumn of 1862, the large civil hospitals of Baltimore, Philadelphia, Pittsburg, New York, Brooklyn, Boston, Cincinnati, Chicago, and St. Louis, were filled to overflowing, and still there was a demand for more. In Washington, nearly all the churches of the city were taken for hospital purposes, and in Philadelphia, several churches were temporarily used for the same purpose. Large private residences and warehouses were for the time being transformed into hospitals. It was stated that there then were 130,000 sick and wounded requiring hospital accommodations. In New York, in addition to the established civil hospitals, the fine building just completed for a Foundling Hospital, on the corner of Fifty-first street and Lexington avenue, and a large building, formerly an arsenal in the Central Park, were tendered to the Government by the city, and the busy hands of the ladies were tasked to furnish the necessary hospital furniture for them.

In Philadelphia a large hospital, with capacity for five hundred beds, on the corner of Broad and Prince streets, was erected and furnished mainly by the efforts and personal labor of the mechanics of the vicinity, much of the labor being performed at night, after the regular toil of the day was done. The Government furnished medical and surgical attendance, nurses, medicines, and rations for the patients, but there was need of changes of clothing, delicacies, food not coming within the rations, but more suitable for the sick; and stationery, postage stamps, papers, &c. These were all furnished by the ready contributions of the citizens, as was the case also in all the military hospitals throughout the country.

As soon as possible the Government erected extensive hospitals, and rented, or accepted where the city authorities or citizens tendered buildings suitable for their purpose, and arranged a system of complete hospitals, on a scale sufficiently large to answer the demands even of the vast army now in the field. Washington has now twenty-two military hospitals, affording accommodation for ten thousand patients ; Baltimore, hospitals for about three thousand ; Philadelphia twenty-six hospitals, with accommodation for thirteen thousand ; Pittsburgh four, with accommodation for three thousand ; the New York and New England department, thirteen, with about nine thousand beds, beside a number of small post hospitals ; St. Louis and vicinity, thirteen, with beds for ten thousand patients, and Floating Hospitals on the Mississippi, accommodations for about the same number. The hospital accommodations at New Orleans, Memphis, Nashville, Louisville, Indianapolis, Cincinnati, Columbus, Cleveland, Chicago, Keokuk, Davenport, and other points in the West, swell the aggregate possible number of beds to nearly, or quite,one hundred and fifty thousand, without again occupying civil hospitals. To all these the contributions of hospital delicacies, clothing, &c., have been and still are, constant, from the Sanitary Commissions, the Christian Commission, Ladies' Aid Societies, and individual donors.

Appendix J.

We have already alluded in this Appendix to some of the abundant instances of personal self-sacrifices for the care of the sick and wounded, but they are so numerous that it is vain to attempt to do justice to all. A few others, however, are specially deserving of honor, from the extent and continuance of their labors. Among these may be named Miss D. L. Dix, so widely known for her labor in behalf of the insane, and who very early in the war undertook, under Government appointment, the superintendence of the hospitals in Washington and its vicinity ; Miss S. M. Powell, of New York, who engaged in similar duties, with a zeal and discretion worthy of the highest praise; Mrs. T. J. Fales, and Miss Clara Barton, who were the pioneers, where many others have since followed, in ministering to the wounded on the battle-field, and whose energy, promptness, and tenderness, as well as their endurance, have won for them the almost idolatrous affection of the soldiers ; Mrs. General Lander, and Miss Fanny D. Gage, who have done so much for the sick and wounded soldiers at Port Royal and vicinity ; the Misses Morrison, also of Washington ; H. M. Pierce, LL. D., of New York, who spent months in hospital superintendence, and in urging upon the Government the establishment of an efficient ambulance service; Mr. C. B. Barclay, of Philadelphia, one of the most eminent citizens of that city, who gave up home, family, and society, to devote himself to the personal service of the sick and wounded soldiers, and in about one year, from means furnished by himself and his friends, contributed over $100,000 in supplies for their comfort ; Mr. S. B. Fales, a well-known art connoisseur, who has been one of the most efficient contributors to, and laborers in, the Union Volunteer Refreshment Saloon in Philadelphia ; Judge J. E. Yeatman, of St. Louis, President of the Western Sanitary Commission, and Hon Mark Skinner, of Chicago, President of the Chicago Branch of the United States Sanitary Commission, both of whom have given themselves wholly and freely to the work of supplying the needs, and providing for the care of the wounded in the Western armies ; Rev. H. A. Reed, and his noble wife, and C. M. Welles, of Washington, D. C, whose labors have been as abundant and their services as arduous, as most of those we have named; and a host of others, nameless here, but to be held in everlasting remembrance of Him who overlooks no deed of charity and love.

www.ingramcontent.com/pod-product-compliance
Lightning Source LLC
Chambersburg PA
CBHW021638270326
41931CB00008B/1068